THE MUSES

-EPIC ODES-

JG FEDERMAN

POET PRESS®

SEATTLE · BOTHELL

POET PRESS®

PO BOX 117

Bothell WA, 98041

Copyright © 2013-2015 JG Federman.

All rights reserved.

TITLE DEVISED BY JG FEDERMAN
COVER & INTERIOR DESIGN BY JG FEDERMAN
WRITTEN BY JG FEDERMAN

Cover Image: Courtesy of the Getty's Open Content Program
Rosalba Carriera (Italian, 1673 - 1757), A Muse, mid-1720s,
Pastel on laid blue paper 31 x 26 cm (12 3/16 x 10 1/4 in.)
The J. Paul Getty Museum, Los Angeles.

The Getty Museum did not endorse this project or participate in its creation. Interior image credits appear on page 61.

POET PRESS is a trademark of Poet Press, LLC.

www.poetpress.com

10 9 8 7 6 5 4 3 2 1

First Edition

Printed in the United States of America
Library of Congress Control Number: 2015941368

ISBN-13: 978-1-940158-05-1 (paperback)
ISBN-10: 1940158052 (paperback)
ISBN-13: 978-1-940158-09-9 (ebook)
ISBN-10: 1940158095 (ebook)

For Julia

CONTENTS

ACKNOWLEDGMENTS

I would like to thank my family for their support; their devotion and sacrifices made this book possible. I am deeply appreciative of the life-long quest for knowledge my Dad cultivated within me. Special thanks to Jared for his engaging conversations and insights. Also, I would like to thank my Mom for instilling a love of the arts in me. Lastly, thank you Julia for being my muse – I am eternally grateful.

"LET THE MUSES DESCEND AND INVOKE PROSE."

— JG FEDERMAN

-THE MUSES-

INTRODUCTION

Hear oh hear that timeless tale?
The odes of fearful vengeance fail;
But none to hear that call unveiled;
A rhythmic song of history's gales.

Who art they, these Muses of song? [5]
The joy of every mortal thorn.
Tis the truth of lyrical melody aloud;
The simple craft that time didst plow.

These Muses seek to take the floor,
Grant their chorus one last roar? [10]
Betwixt the very hour of late?
Hast granted us love's own estate.

Nine to close the minds of all;
The daughters of Zeus and Mnemosyne enthrall.
Known for their guise of historical notes; [15]
Each wasted letter of scribbled quotes.

O

-ODE 1-

CLIO (HISTORY)

What doth be thy guise Oh Muse?
Be that what it may to lose.
Open thy scroll and tell aloud,
Of seated books and chests unbound. [20]

Dwell with me on the clouds of Olympus?
Amongst the crags and clefts of tempests.
Tis the family of Muse the poetry to define;
Divine ethereal where dost thou lie?

Though the titans didst clamber – [25]
And beckon me after.
Thou didst call the courts of old;
To unfurl the scroll of centuries' gold.

Nay dear one, thou fell for another;
In operatic fashion thou didst mother. [30]
Hymenaeus was borne from thee dear Clio –
The lair of cosmic heaven's Leo.

Second born, dost thou not rest?
Crazed forms of brazen breasts.
Thou sought to tease Aphrodite's heart – [35]
Cast into love with Magnes' son Pieros.

Borne Hyacinthus, a new son of man –
Dost thou now pour out thy sweetness?
Queen of my song will thou play on?
Tis the honor of love to delight in song. [40]

What be thy history of valor?
For only those who sing know her pallor.
Nay the grandiose forms of plans expose;
The empathic chord of villainous prose.

Dost full skill measure thy crown? [45]
The striking haunt of caped resound?
In thy lyre of love men are found wanting sex;
As thou poured out thy spirit of conquest.

Tis the resource of prose only thou knows;
Sing to the Muses of history's clothes. [50]
Honor to wed the forms of clouds –
Ethereal truth to voices goes.

Pride before the fall in tempest keeps;
Doth honor thee in time-tested fate?
The throne of love thou sits upon; [55]
In the sweet, sweet waters of earthen tones.

Flowering words that pass through the ages;
Undaunted by time's immovable sanctum.
Illustrious crimes to gaze upon?
The crimson hues of prayers are born. [60]

Speak again so that I may hear –
Where thou hast gone and I hath been.
The ripened form of prince's tears;
Comely arts amidst these fears.

For the poets sing of thee dear Clio – [65]
Encomia to all life's stories.
Bestow upon me that great glory?
Tis the praise of thee I seek to stay.

What doth be thy aptitude dear one?
To sing the harmonies of fate? [70]
In the shrine of thy heart, or Apollo's tower –
To heave the waters of libations' hour.

Ardent, at best, the conquest of love?
The Muse of principled questions thee.
Art fragrant waters the fragments of thy heart? [75]
Broken pieces of spiritual enclaves.

Tis the ambrosial cave that prays aloud?
To save thee from a sense of drought.
Thou art my Muse of historical prose –
The only form that mankind knows. [80]

Will my winds come to be?
Will thou let them flee?
Like shattered dreams etched away?
With the ink of blood that men hath paid.

What storied annals hast thou passed? [85]
Clipped and prodded for journey's test?
In the realms of the mind thou knows indeed –
Secrets of life to envelop me.

In the force of years thou found clandestineness;
In the mild tongues of lover's presents. [90]
To the truths of courage still denied –
The forms of earth now gently tie.

The weaving threads of pure olfaction;
In the twisting words of ceaseless fractions.
Denote dear love that hopeless attraction – [95]
That seeks to bring this sweet subtraction.

For all men wish to be with thee –
Inscribed in thy scroll of poetry.
History be the great unknown;
To read again the words thou told. [100]

Blessings be the nurtured form –
Of treks for long-lost poems.
In the arts thou found the greatest clues;
To hand to earth's undaunted dew.

Claim the force of upward prose? [105]
Heroic let the consonants crow.
Tis the memories of love to fade?
In the melodies of time's parade.

Nay dear Clio thou still resides;
Among the fervent desires of mind. [110]
In retrospect the titans claimed –
Thy voice of love and spirited praise.

As the rippling waters flow from Greece;
Let all the springs and wells now taste.
The grandest form of reworked stone; [115]
The scrolls of human history told.

Hear now the Muse of the mortal ages!
Gentle grace of passing fate.
The beauteous form of natural wonder –
For all to behold and subject themselves under. [120]

Bend the notes and break the yolks;
The cattle farms and beaches quote.
From wars and hate thy military forsakes;
The pen and ink her magistrate.

Forge forever that new estate? [125]
In that most holy, reverent place.
For soon the world will burn untamed;
Will thy scroll so to be claimed?

The blackened forms of life once stood;
In the fires of life thou understood. [130]
As parchment flutters in the breeze
The roaring flames of upmost ease.

Charred and broken it will drain;
As life grants each moment's pain.
In the grieving words of loveless hornets; [135]
The grandest force is that of chorus.

O

-ODE 2-

URANIA (ASTRONOMY)

What doth be the silver star of night?
That creaks and daunts with day?
Urania thou art heavenly bright;
The blistering force of cosmic entrees. [140]

Detail the painting of cosmic love?
Thou alone dost know whereof.
From whence didst little Linus spawn?
Where the globe of lofty heights was drawn.

Fixed attention – doth it reside in the clouds? [145]
Of futures seen in cosmic skies.
Tell of that arranged spark –
In nebulas' homes of garden locks.

Universal love dost thou not know?
The epic ode of spiritual ties. [150]
For heavenly notes now garb thy throne;
Dressed in cloaks of stars and chrome.

For I concern myself with philosophy's kin;
The taste of all below her whim.
If not but a thousand suns to burn; [155]
The Muse of thee Urania to spurn.

Tis the lyre of life diffused this day?
Each hour of cosmic entity.
To burn aloft in purest fury,
The grander forms of loving beauty. [160]

Exalted now the call will fly;
In the swelling tempest of the mind.
And begin to roll in the halls of Jove –
The ceaseless wonder of celestial orbs,

Tis meaning that poets ask of thee? [165]
Striking not their fancy falls –
For I call to thee, thy name alone;
To craft for me this verse of love.

What writing dost thou infuse?
In the subtle reaches of global hues. [170]
Each guise to wear the rod affixed –
In heavenly ties of whimsy spirit.

For I know that thou alone didst wake;
With silver cakes adorned in space.
As thy lyre rules the cosmic strand – [175]
The chorus of unbelievable ends.

Who dost thou now assess?
This gift of poetry pressed and sent;
Sublime in nature and violet crowns;
Adorn the love of mindless sounds. [180]

Where hast thy headband gone?
Of flittered gold and woven song.
That flooded the fields of Elysium with prose;
Those heavenly gates thou alone didst storm.

For distinguished speech alone dost raise – [185]
The flimsy excuse of torrent rage.
What be the hymn Urania this day?
In subtle whims thou contemplates.

As each grasshopper informs thee of mortal death;
Honor men above these insects? [190]
Art thou not concerned with power and thought?
The divine inspiration of uttered constructs.

Tis imagination thy greatest gift?
Unseeing heights of each soul to lift.
In gratuities' beat of civil unrest; [195]
The tempest of creation's test.

What hast thou to say of Corymbus of Helicon?
Former friends didst thou disarm?
To preside over one in Stygian ways;
And predict ones death with starlit pleas. [200]

For as Linus commanded the harpists and singers;
Even in death he transcended ages.
And Phoibos bled the hunted waste;
Of vengeful tales and ominous estates.

Hymenaios fell to Moira's hands; [205]
Didst thou not wail at this lament?
Didst the Muses mourn at the loss of their own?
To the world of intuitive mortal groans.

Their tongues, dear Urania, didst they wave?
In the war of Dionysos, thou sought to save. [210]
Despite the water's coarse display;
The grapes of wrath where war is laid.

Speak now dear Urania to the earth's inhabitants;
With declarations of haughty balance.
For in striking form they seek to shout – [215]
In crowded displays of anguished maze.

Level against the crumbs of sages –
The wooden vessel of Jason's praise.
Tis the Argonaut of love poetry remains?
In the esteemed reaches of universal glades. [220]

The golden forms dost thou not take?
From the trees of heaven's stately gate.
Fired bronze of glorious thrones –
The brazen fight of Apollo's own.

Demonstrate the return of the Muses? [225]
For all mortals to consume.
Alight this page with hopeful dreams;
And ink the space now void today.

Where will life be found Urania?
When millennia pass, where will thou be? [230]
Beside the hopes of dreamy worlds;
The savagery death behooves the word.

Reply to the chorus of thy sisters;
In beckoned beauty they revealed.
The estranged tongue of broken praise; [235]
For new gods have taken hold of grace.

What now takes hold of featured flight?
In truest tales of odious fashion.
For Olympian forms cannot compete –
To the words of love that astronomy beats. [240]

Hast thou heard the slumber of the cosmos?
Seen the birth of righteous stars?
The beginning of life Urania knows;
Will thou release a glimpse of prose?

For the glee of life bears witness thee; [245]
Each practice of watching endlessly.
Observe the talent thou displayed?
In fettered harmonies of days.

As the vast expanse of space draws near;
To a close my dear · the page is filled. [250]
With inken prose the heavens unfurled;
To the lavish sound of thy harp's world.

Betwixt the sense of upmost ease –
That resonates so passionately.
Be the angel of heroic prose? [255]
That tunes of songs of humanity's own.

Art the heavens like Argos' speckled form?
The glittering strands of silvered ease.
As thou sits shrouded in a blanket of night;
With airy parts and starry heights. [260]

For as each Muse waits in ethereal towers;
The odes of song will fill their rafters.
For even the immortals must sing a tune;
To the dance of love and endless dew.

O

-ODE 3-

MELPOMENE (TRAGEDY)

Famed tragedy dost thou resound? [265]
Cruel and inhumane torture abounds.
The remains of mortal lives that sailed;
Languished over such haunted tales.

Hast thou found the course of mortal ways?
Sought the end of death's own stinging praise? [270]
For who sings to thee if not lament?
Those that seek to unearth distress.

Behooved the mix of twisted fates –
Where harmonies invoke that taste;
In comedic song will thy tragedy resound? [275]
To revert the sense of joyous crowds.

Nay in the battles of the mind –
Each prisoner will ultimately find.
The creative sense of nature's plea –
For mortals to invest in thee. [280]

For song and dance be the meaning of thee;
Why art thou now tragedy's crown?
To celebrate is the epitome of thee;
Art thou not frightened at what thou will be?

Where art thy boots of tragic song? [285]
Cothurnus to drive the tragedy home!
Hold thy club aloft and stone;
The knife thou wields when the stage is gone.

Tis the mask thou holds to show appeal –
To the audience in case the rhythms fail. [290]
Adorn thou dost a crown of cypress;
Or ivy my dear dost thou caress?

Implore thee Muse · rhyme this verse!
And forge a beautiful moment of length.
Create a sense of lyrical praise – [295]
On this voyage of love and merchant graves.

Celebrate now with the attitude of zeal;
As thou didst spawn the Seirenes.
Intuitive fashion, thou dost protest.
The straining voice of music's theft. [300]

Yet men doth wish to lay with thee –
In the chanting forms of melodies.
For only thou canst charm the mind;
As listening ears fall to thy plight.

Tis that ruse which convinced the River Achelous? [305]
Subtlety touching and probing his pockets.
While thou gathered ivy for the thyrsus – wand;
Along the shores of his banks in ethereal bond.

Anoint the mystic drops of dew –
From flowers beyond the range of Zeus. [310]
And rains above the realm of Apollo;
To infuse the earth with mature followers.

From thy lips the curse of celebration exists;
For all participate in grandeur bliss.
The revelry that forces the cosmic twist – [315]
The subliminal speech thou loftily kissed.

Measure the gifts of Melpomene?
For they are not abundant.
Her gentle smile charms and plays –
And shall rise again when curtain's display. [320]

Who hast seen the course of her hours?
Sat and watched her craft each actors' prowess.
For to ask this Muse for grace and rest;
Behooved this sense of loneliness!

What dost thou require Melpomene? [325]
In sins committed beside thee.
What can mortals do when life fades away?
Besides sing the music of hopeless flames?

What is worth noting in spite of comedy?
The tragedy of plays in Grecian days. [330]
For authorities cower in banquet halls;
To hear odes of glorious battle songs.

Reclaim dear Muse this poetical song!
And heed thy sister's elegant prose.
In wretched thickets of disaster it strikes; [335]
Tragic is the music that fights.

In the summoning winds of war tis made;
The unworn melody of praise.
Like babbling brooks envelop thee –
Commence the forceful prints of peace. [340]

On stage dear Muse thou creates drama;
Will thou not help each poet's persona?
Confer the strokes of melodious ease –
Upon this parchment prepared for thee.

What canst a mortal give to convince thee? [345]
No earthly present sufficiently woos thee.
If writing a song thou requires me –
How canst my wishes surpass those of many?

Hunted prose only thou will know;
Where Melpomene stalks thee in these woods! [350]
For the words of life will soon concede –
The battered sense of justly pleas.

Relish the envy of the comedy's luster?
The laughter that fills bowls of custard.
For in the rosy passion Melpomene finds – [355]
A way inside the human mind.

Be rid of her wit?
Nay, for smiles demand that spirit.
For the chorus will delight at the sound of her voice.
As the audience cringes at the plight of each choice. [360]

What can be given to such a Muse?
To invoke the passion of ink's own swirls?
For to move the soul and change its course;
The storms of life will rip in two.

A soul to bargain for thy passage? [365]
Safely across the forceful waters of Hades.
Tis in the weeping forms of prose I wait;
To cast thee off, oh tragedy of fate!

-ODE 4-

THALIA (COMEDY)

Flourishing Muse dost thou break out?
Like thy sister Melpomene, will thou resound? [670]
Tis the comedic form of life to stand?
To sing praises and poems at love's demand.

Bucolic poetry, dost thou know her name?
Amidst the actors who profess their fame.
In the festivities of life each flower blooms; [675]
Within the fields of Elysium's vital swoons.

What dost thou hold in thy hands dear one?
The comic mask and shepherd's staff.
Adorned the ivy dons thy head –
The silvery throat of God's own band. [680]

Didst thou with Apollo forge the Korybantes?
Or craft from heaven's hands that thread.
Of tapestry's bright with rhythms of rhyme;
Flourish dear Thalia in the plains of time.

Why is thy hand upon thy face? [685]
As thou stands against these pillars of fate.
In whispered tones the vibrations ring;
And in honeyed voice thy passion sings.

Summon me to that grand court above;
With humbled skies of staged delight. [690]
To the course of history thou imparts –
Golden melodies of love's own heart.

What couldst the mortals learn from thee?
Perhaps tame forms of prose?
Give in to the sense of untold drawls; [695]
The lessons only thou composed.

What dost thou demonstrate in time?
If comedy were to find her rhyme.
In the darkened corridors of the mind –
For immortal sages now are blind. [700]

What teaches us dear Thalia of laughter?
Tis the sounds of glorious banter?
Or the joyful ode in gestured hours;
In the vital stance of emerging towers.

Where dost thou spend thy days? [705]
Away in solace for the thinking age;
With eyes affixed on the horizon –
The purple futures of crimson brightens.

Will thou call the audience tonight?
And let the sumptuous revelry alight? [710]
Tis the playful aria of notes thou told;
In forlorn tongues of blistering cold.

With the flowers tossed at thy feet dear Thalia;
Dost thou watch them wither?
Roses left to be trampled and cleft; [715]
When thou leaves the stage with a life to lead.

For the human condition requires no faction;
Or simple plays of satisfaction.
Tis the wondrous breath nature displays –
When all manner of ghastly ghosts are slain. [720]

In the horrors of night thou alone concludes;
Their dismal end when sounds consume.
The laughter of jovial life –
Thou wages against the forms of strife.

Comfort us comedy and heal our wounds! [725]
Protect us from the dying world.
For in the realms of happenstance thou hast trapped;
The bitter end of lives men clasped.

For the show moves on and closes down;
Ending again to the beat of one sound. [730]
As the audience leaves and actors abandon –
That stage of prose and happy quotes.

Will thou, oh Muse, respect this plea –
And invoke the necessity of thee?
For comedy be more than trivial laughs; [735]
Her vital form entrances dance.

So the mortals cry in halls above;
The rapturous cheers of joyful doves.
Where gods can feel the piercing blows –
Of memorable dialogue that forges gold. [740]

Fictitious is this silvery tongue?
That graces the heart of mortal drums.
In lengthy regions of despair –
Only thou canst save love from her lair.

Will thou hear it now? [745]
While the prose of poetry quietly astounds
To shake the earth's foundations down –
And lie awake in revelry's fountain.

In quaking fashion, all too easy;
This Muse creates such dignity. [750]
Wouldst thou fill the void of white?
For upon this page lies golden night.

The return of happy, exuberant tones,
Who will they be loaned?
What becomes of the songs of old? [755]
That tame the beasts of the underworld's throne.

Fragrant art the words of many?
Who seek to spurn thee inconsequently.
In gardens of beauty thou stands true;
The ultimate price of ticketed swoon. [760]

This call goes up to the Muse Thalia;
To fill the work of poetry's duties.
For all to read and so construct;
The veracious withering so abrupt.

Will thou, oh Muse, free the silence? [765]
In burning realms of fleeting presence.
For the audience lies in wait for thee;
To preserve the faith of mortality.

So call that name and beckon her hither;
Like the serpent's tempting form didst slither. [770]
Is a verse of thee pure luminosity?
Forever etched eternally.

-ODE 5-

TERPSICHORE (DANCE)

Muse of song will thou sing?
With thy lyre of artistic streams;
And the plectrum of starlit praise. [775]
Which grant the hymns of odious days.

Summon the chorus of nature!
For the great halls of the kings await.
Win for all the honor of the earth?
For I will trade thee the husk of Argos. [780]

Rosy goddess, didst thou delight in good things?
Even education's beat and deathless wings?
For thy disciple grants all mortal dreams;
In recitation's beautiful, bountiful beams.

Hail the futures of music's form – [785]
As pages ripped in times torn.
The dance of lore from her be told;
Terpsichore, the mortals hope to unfold.

Grant the case of staged delights?
For the audience demands thy exquisite sight. [790]
Envisioned lofty Olympus this hour?
With a harp that conducts thee louder.

The course of prose in movement's wake;
Rare form indeed – of dreamy states.
Tis the daughters of dance to fill the sky? [795]
On earth and space, and every eye.

Terpsichore, the dance's score;
What hast thou heard sung before?
In nature's hands of ravenous ways;
The dancing moonlight of each wave. [800]

What dost thou feature Muse?
In passion for mortals to choose.
What befalls each viewer's means?
Beyond that of melodious strings.

Enraptured notions of equal stones; [805]
Where oh Muse hast thou belonged?
For stars with golden threads doth weave;
The fleece of lore and dreamy dreams.

Invite life, dear Muse, into thy court;
For the penalty of succulent dance was bought. [810]
What trills began the steps again?
And cast thee to the frenzy of music's bed.

Indeed, thou art, the Muse of priceless sense;
That invigorated passion requests.
In the hills of Elysium, dost thou rest? [815]
For I write of thee Muse to ease this test.

Where doth the fiery cackles falter?
In each stage of life and dewless water.
My chest dost wait for thee to fly;
As the chorus begins to rise on high. [820]

Hast thou wept in front of hordes?
As battered eyes blink teary shores.
The salty odes of rapturous scores;
In life doth they guard against rewards.

What dost thou level against the gods of old? [825]
Hasten vixen of thrones unknown.
To worlds seen only with the stages' code;
The call to arms in rhythmic prose.

Terpsichore the dance completes the floor.
Will thou lead the final score? [830]
Into the depths of reaching thorns;
The bright morn of yellowed horns.

For life hast tried to slow thy wake.
Icy stares and cold, cold drakes,
In heaven's tales thou overcame – [835]
The Titan hordes of Hade's gleam.

Dance on dear Muse, dance on!
Tis the music of thee my own reward.
Intuitively raise the call to arms;
For all to meet thee in thy charm. [840]

In fame's estate thou now resides;
Wouldst thou let me but pry?
For the rhythm of all lies in the stars;
The movement of the cosmos seen from afar.

Dance once more for the earth to see; [845]
Thy great and noble chivalry.
For goddesses liken the form of thee;
Entranced in golden memories.

Art thou the sweet olfaction Terpsichore?
For few have written satire of thee before. [850]
The eye's treat, art thou not amused?
For mortal minds remain confused.

Engrained in the heart's own fire;
Thou hast branded love's desire.
In the forged lava of the soul; [855]
For all to recite and forever know.

Hast thou grasped the intricacies of song?
For mortal music is the art of form.
The dance it claims for its own sake;
To cut off the chains of lazy weight. [860]

For I hath watched thee dance;
Terpsichore, thou didst entrance.
The steps were created long ago;
Before the world was even known.

Where in the darkness was the dance? [865]
Choreographed bliss thou sought to prance.
That composed sense of melodious ascent;
In tune with holy, cosmic sense.

Tis the music of thee I hath in mind;
To bring a light from darker times. [870]
Resist not the creation of lore;
For Terpsichore hast rekindled war.

-ODE 6-

CALLIOPE (EPIC POETRY)

Who dost this Muse now seek?
    In the epic forms of poetry's beat;
    What be the temptation to overcome? [875]
When all things bright and beautiful art done.

Eldest Muse where dost thou be?
Goddess of poetry bestow life to me!
To silence the whimsy, chains of burdens;
In the eloquent fields of prudent burgeons. [880]

What dost thou hold aloft in feminine wiles?
A lyre or tablet of striking style?
On the scroll of heart, thy epic sense –
The poetic justice of sentience.

Where art the songs of thy own son; [885]
Tis the harp of Orpheus now a stone?
Didst thou recover the music of verse?
To usher in heaven's birth?

Nine were the notes of his lyre;
Nine the number of sister Muses. [890]
On Olympus thou stood, garbed in verse –
On every lip and human curse.

As the Bakkhantes tore Orpheus –
Didst thou tear these pages of earth?
When thou recovered his head to enshrine; [895]
On the isle of Lesbos to redefine.

Orpheus son of Oeagrus and thee;
Where doth the golden sword now gleam?
Poetic praise to speak of thee;
In sultry hours of honeyed sweets. [900]

Didst Eurydice quell his tortured soul?
When the lyre of his prose laid cold.
Into the depths of Hades it fell –
The tempest keep of vicious hell.

Descriptive notions, will they cease? [905]
If blooming thorns of meadows speak.
Of petals fallen in the wood –
Against the grains of lover's food.

Lovely-haired goddess, what dost thou assume?
In the poetic musings of swoony bosom. [910]
Thou took a Thrakian near the heights of Pimplea;
And bore a son to shake the stony waters of earth free.

Hast the quotations from many eluded thee?
Of epic poems so ripe with greed.
With their plagiarized forms of mass absurdity; [915]
They call upon Hade's dark obscenities.

For me dear Calliope the stage is set;
The voyage across the relentless tempest.
Precept's verse of ink displayed –
Marked against the page's days. [920]

As the poet's pen slows the draft –
So life is finally past.
To grant the quest of literary love.
The eternal world of golden doves.

As Homer appealed to thy very nature; [925]
Who dost best the journey thou creates?
Even modern tongues will fade away –
Against the darkened veil of Hades.

But thou lives on sweet Calliope;
Despite the arduous existence spent. [930]
To show the universe life's own message –
A cosmic verse of convalescence.

Labored sounds of written notes;
Against the parchment ink invokes.
A beautiful glow of human words; [935]
The precious testament gods will learn.

Hast the heavens read of thee dear Muse?
In swirling fashion they imbue distractions.
Proving naught but the climbing soul –
A poem written for thee alone. [940]

Didst a torrent of letters convince thee?
Surely thou meant to receive these.
Or art thou the cause of many poems?
That sought to capture essential tones.

Calliope dost thou deliver us? [945]
In the trials of ink and humble sports.
The legends of man and ages dawn;
With the glittering arms of pens adorned.

Will thou not spread the word?
To free the tones of epic concern; [950]
And emancipate the soul's darkened days;
In the forms of praise the gods awake.

Hast the heavens opened, dear Muse, this hour?
Flooding trenches to feed the bowers?
The taste of earth and sentient days; [955]
Invoke the fruits of lovely praise.

To bear the truth of inks' one course;
Appeal to the life that wrote each verse?
The slowing hand of mind and body;
That commands the voice of gifted hobbies. [960]

Didst thou receive a mortal gift?
The unwavering book gentility lifts.
Despite the onslaught of waning wings –
The angelic beat of poetry sings.

Each quivered tongue soon to wake; [965]
Didst thou not speak of fate?
For the wisest of each Muse be thee;
In the stories of prose thou relays to me.

Upon rosy waters of the earth;
The perilous streams of every verse; [970]
In epic poems and tales of woe;
Be the heroes of old and Calliope's prose.

O

-ODE 7-

ERATO (LOVE POETRY)

For who charms the sight –
   In virtue's plight?
   Erato who doth be? [975]
   The whimsical nature of infidelity.

On the mount doth all hear?
Draw close to me goddess without any fear;
   For the words of affection –
Seek to upend and command attention. [980]

Art thy words of grace the notes of love?
Victorious in death and commander of doves;
   Be the truth of vision's airy eyes;
For souls doth weep when faced with lies.

Desired Muse be mine forever? [985]
Beneath the lovely heavens pleasure.
The invocation each soul raptures on high;
As the suggested voice of love doth rise;

Upon thy head the roses shiver;
To sing the songs of loves delivered. [990]
In the wreath of myrtle flowers whispered;
Didst thou devise Kithara's treasures?

Call the lords of cosmic cause;
Voice the earnest law of all.
Pick up the lyre thou invented – [995]
To sing the hymns unprecedented.

Beloved Muse and flower of love;
Thy call behooves the gentle rose.
Art thou the mimic imitation?
Bestowed from Olympus to destroy division. [1000]

Satiate love, what dost thou desire?
In tired forms of hearts aspired.
Where is thy tomb Erato;
On the island of Samos where stars are born?

In the times of Pausanias, lovers crossed – [1005]
Raging seas of hellish force.
For thou to grant such a Grecian fate;
Remains the nature of airy flames.

Didst thou wed Malos, Lord of Malea?
What of thy daughter Cleophema? [1010]
Didst she take Phelegyas of Epidauros;
To wrap Aigle in starry shawls?

When Apollo took Aigle didst thou relent?
Their child Asclepius dismissed torment.
Erato art the Muse of time's desire; [1015]
The worthiness of love's undying lyre.

Amidst the clouds of shrinking grey –
Grand beings come out to play.
Of rich, rich schemes and pleasant beams;
The moonlit strands of silver streams. [1020]

Aloft the garb of heaven's verse;
The gift that soulful churches purse.
The tumult cries in bed delights –
The virtues that night alone defines.

Wherein the hearts of heaven and home; [1025]
Doth the sensual sounds of joy abound?
With goddesses that bare their naked forms;
To the sweet, sweet longings of honeyed storms.

In the wordy breaths of charity's odes;
Each life finds nature inside a rose. [1030]
As the erotic tongues of era's fall –
Among the burning pages of history's walls.

In the flames of cupid's quivered fires;
Thou bore the garden of luscious choirs.
With mirrored words and lovely satire; [1035]
Those suited forms of golden attire.

In gilded metals so adorned –
Wouldst thou quell the thirst that was forewarned?
For thou alone hast beauty bestowed;
Unchanging as the sea's Calypso. [1040]

Billowing roars of each kisses' waves;
The oceanic score of that never aged.
Tis within the rhymes of feminine wiles;
The soul will wake to win its smiles.

Hast thou heard the whispers of Grecian shores? [1045]
Where battles raged and hearts implored.
At night they beckon within dreamy halls;
While kings of earth waged war on all.

To open starlight and honeyed dew;
The flowers red and colored hues. [1050]
That passion places in the mind;
To ignite the heart and pleasure time.

Hath the days been enough?
Amongst the crags and streams of silver bluffs.
For infinity itself will never suffice; [1055]
In the mind's delights of forests bright.

Tis the beginning of fervor Erato?
In that zealous curse of jewels.
For infatuation thou dost use –
To entrance them all in lavish Muse. [1060]

Yes, thou dost draw the canopy of night;
The stunning winds of seduced flight.
Where the stars avail the crimson hues –
Of lover's hearts and minds renewed.

So hold aloft the arrow of love; [1065]
Tis in the words of poetry ink will clothe.
To inspire all the grandest prose;
The torch of hearts and souls alone.

Human ears hath learned to belong;
To the sense's fate in love's own song. [1070]
With the beating rush of quivering aim;
I am the fallen stag of woodland fame.

-ODE 8-

POLYHYMNIA
(SONGS TO THE GODS)

Didst thou have an angle love?
In the Muse of song thou laid above.
For where doth the amateur lie? [1075]
In sweet delights of praise to thee.

The form of those divine hymns;
The sacred poetry of heavenly whims.
The pantomime, Polyhymnia, didst thou sing?
For tis thou alone who invented geometry. [1080]

In thy strict forms, dear deity –
Hair wrapped in wreathes of Daphne.
The soul's expressions towards the sky –
Filled with thy music of the lyre.

What dost thou contemplate? [1085]
In thy leaning stature of sculpted fate.
Thy thoughts alone to comfort thee;
Dear Muse of song play on to me.

For what dost this in poetry display?
What the grand truth of lyrics make. [1090]
The intense songs of love's own capture;
Sinking tunes of glorious rapture.

In the endless songs of praise to thee;
Muse of music sing on to me.
Develop prose of perfect pitch – [1095]
In harmonious verse thou lives in spirit.

Who doth greet and worship thee?
Dear Polyhymnia thou commands the seas.
In the endless songs of praises to thee;
This voyage continues in whispered ease. [1100]

Where didst thou first strike chorus?
In the angelic realms of soulful forests.
Tis truth of notes, Polyhymnia to dine;
At the table of love with cups of wine.

For in highest heaven the sounds doth ring; [1105]
In caressing tones of pleasant odes.
That thou hast made in sweet delight;
To appease the earth and gods with might.

Play on dear Muse and bar the chords –
Of joyous tremolos and hopeful scores! [1110]
Tis the notes of life thou rectified;
To raise the roofs of shackled heights.

Hast thou received the gifts of nectar?
The honeyed words of sweetest vector.
For thou described the angles of love – [1115]
In married forms of triangle's folds.

Tis abstract dear Muse to assume the latter?
Forget not the songs of heaven's battles.
For aloft it soars in legends untold;
The words of praise and courage bold. [1120]

If mortal tongues doth wake this hour;
In happy homes and higher towers.
What dost thou give men of earnest speak?
Against the silvery threads that Hades weaves.

Or the titans of Greece, dear Muse, that war; [1125]
Will thou not hold the trumpet call?
Against the backdrop of starry nights –
The endless scenes of bloody rites.

Greatest Muse thou devised simple equations;
To measure love and the science of invasion. [1130]
Against the artful forms of cold abrasion;
Thou stomped the hearts of those occasions.

Will thou hold thy lyre aloft?
And guide the course of billions of songs.
If tongues of mortals sought evasion; [1135]
It was thou who captured them in the art of persuasion.

For the delight of life hast fallen to thee;
Polyhymnia at last the world is free!
To worship loud and fervent still;
The beating drums of the god's own will. [1140]

Into the depths of sweetest praise;
The hearts of mortals spend their days.
In the sunny skies of each cloudless night;
Thou swoons the lyre's strings with light.

Tis in written prose the hymns disguise; [1145]
Against the veil of drawing night.
Tis the wisest of Muses to sing of gods?
The words of love that thanks be of.

Usher in the dance of tones?
For assuredly thou alone must know. [1150]
In Olympus tales of legends resound;
But none like the hymns of Polyhymnia's mouth.

If reaching expanse guided thee far;
Wouldst the prose of mortal tongues find that star?
How wouldst thou entrance the cosmos? [1155]
In their delicate dance of silent Zeus.

Tis golden strings thou plucks this day?
To seduce the woodlands and the glades.
Admit the grandeur of thy hymns;
For every earth and mortal sin. [1160]

To reach the chasms of the mind;
The music thou makes hast so defined.
A glorious sound to maintain respect;
In the awesome powers of cosmic presence.

Where hast thou endeavored still? [1165]
In the joys of words that music fills.
To the scripted notes of inken prose;
Relish the smell of rosy odes.

For each Muse hath brought a reason to love;
But thou Polyhymnia hast a reason above! [1170]
On the order of billions her songs rise;
Into the expanse of bright blue brilliant skies.

-ODE 9-

EUTERPE (LYRIC POETRY)

Dost thou not administer delight?
Oh Muse of song play on this night!
For thy song and dance Euterpe design; [1175]
And probe the catacombs of mortal minds.

For thy music alone surpasses the heavens;
Outstretched in hymns of glorious severance.
Giver of delight, wouldst thou free me?
In the spheres of lyrical poetry. [1180]

For thy double-flute hast charmed my ears;
Even Grecian heroes doth rest their spears.
To listen to the Muse of Olympus enchant;
The multitudes of mortal army's hands.

For thy mother, Mnemosyne, bore thee dear one; [1185]
And brought forth the sweetest sounds.
To dance and sing the prose of epics;
The odyssey love, thou perfected its relic.

Didst thou lay with the river Strymon?
To bear Rhesus, the name of thy spawn. [1190]
In the depths of Troy he coldly fell;
By Diomedes' hand in darkened hell.

For thou dear Muse art most comely;
Fighting forces that make men glum.
What is the mortal appropriation of thee? [1195]
The terrapin love, that only thou can sing.

Euterpe, thou ministers in the sweetest way;
Tis education thou bestows in grace.
In every temple of marbled stone;
The test of time is passed with song. [1200]

For every Grecian heart and home;
Thou alone hast seen the artful tone.
Of crafted delight of crimson rites –
In purist fashion thou rewrites.

The figures of each Muse are surely enchanting; [1205]
At Pieria they are worshiped on high with chanting.
What leaves this place for all mortals to hear?
A golden boat laden with gifts of cheer.

Gifts of verse and prose for all;
For Greece listens to only one goddesses' song. [1210]
Tis the words of Euterpe herself that ring;
True to the legends she envelops with strings.

Tis vibrant sounds of heaven that speak?
The shards of love and sultry sweets.
Play dear Muse, play on forever! [1215]
In the hearts and minds of mortal endeavors.

Beyond the tales of titan's woes;
Hercules' triumphs or Jason's shores.
The heroes Euterpe lie in thy eyes –
With each word of praise thou sings at night. [1220]

Who but thou hast guided remembrance?
Across millennia for iconic reverence.
For eons mankind will remember thy songs –
With each generation's joyful throngs.

Now board that treasured ship of past – [1225]
And dream within the words that Euterpe cast.
Tis in the realms of divine delights;
The Muses of nine enrapture the night.

To relish the fate of dreamy towers;
As gods alike concede their power. [1230]
Within each song and dance forever –
Bring forth the lyrics of charming endeavors.

Hast thou dear Muse convinced the sages?
Amongst the stars and mortal ages.
Tis in the lofty heights of space; [1235]
The delights of prose be thy lovely face.

So bear witness to the strength of all –
Who toiled within Greece's walls!
The glee that trumpets for centuries more –
In the epic poetry adored. [1240]

Thou hast sent us cupid's quiver –
The single arrow of delightful silver.
To fill the hearts of love's before –
And see the story of heroes restored.

Tis the golden apples and fleece they gained; [1245]
With fires burned and titans slain.
The poetic forms of journey's made –
Retold for centuries in serenades.

Euterpe thou implores music's use;
To drink the god's own divine juice. [1250]
Now sing the choired, angelic hymn –
Of hero's lost and battles grim.

For all to drink the nectar of prose;
Only poetry bears the fruit exposed.
In epic words the hand hast writ – [1255]
A final word of courageous fit.

An empty verse of blackened ink;
Those chains of love that thou hast linked.
Laid out upon pages of powdered pink;
Retouch the verse when pentameter blinks. [1260]

Where doth wisdom lay within her shrine?
The one and only iambic sign.
Tis thee dear Muse that poetry ensues;
Within the sense's life of mystic clues.

In the voyage of delight Euterpe survives; [1265]
The final Muse that willingly dives.
Below the oceans of the mind –
To cast her last and final line.

So sail that treasured ship at last –
Filled with songs and happy chants. [1270]
Across the seas of silken eternity;
Dear Muse, Euterpe, thou hast smitten me.

"MUSE, THOU ART MINE BUT FOR A MOMENT."

— JG FEDERMAN

-THE MUSES-

END

At last thou hast paid homage to them all –
Grecian loves of Olympian halls;
Harmonious life for those that choose –[1275]
Patron saints of creativity's Muse.

Antiquity's hour reigns supreme;
Joyous musings a recurrent theme;
A history carved upon its walls –
Of science and art, knowledge calls! [1280]

Nine beauties born for inspiration;
Granting dreams hewn from aspiration;
Doth they explore caverns of thy imagination?
Yes, for each Muse invokes innovation!

Nine lovely daughters embody thee; [1285]
Dear knowledge thou enraptures me!
Thy ode eclipses the cosmic score –
Producing wondrous celestial décor.

Dear Muses! Grant the words of wisdom wings;
Songs of knowledge to forever sing; [1290]
Please lift the gentle chorus of prose aloft;
Beyond the scope of mortal thought.

Pour waters of ingenuity into our souls –
So we may honor thee in life's inked scroll;
Light the fuse and ignite our minds; [1295]
Forever thy gifts remain enshrined!

Eloquent Muse thou art favored;
Proclaim the history of mankind's labor!
For in each heart lives a rose of truth;
Pleasure masked with honeyed youth. [1300]

A flute for thee to stir the heavens –
With sacred hymns of luminescence;
To dance oh Muse thou knows it best –
A comedy of life so blessed.

Emerge once more gentle Muses of lore; [1305]
And let the peaceful histories roar;
For thee the earth appears aloft;
Against spattered stars and worlds uncrossed.

First Line Index

Photo Credits

Interior images: Courtesy of the Getty's Open Content Program: Dupasquier, Antoine-Léonard (~1748-1832), Sketchbook of Roman antiquities, pen and ink, pencil, wash (1779).

About the Author

JG Federman is an award-winning educator and poet. He is the author of *Art: Quotations of Inspiration*, *Posthumous Examinations* and *Leadership Quotations for Success*. Mr. Federman has been published in scholarly journals for his academic work and writes the "Featured Plant" article for a local botanical garden. He has several forthcoming titles to be published by Poet Press.

The Muses

POET PRESS®

WWW.POETPRESS.COM

PO Box 117 · Bothell · WA · 98041

www.ingramcontent.com/pod-product-compliance
Lightning Source LLC
Chambersburg PA
CBHW021220020426
42331CB00003B/389